SHH, WE'RE ~~NOT~~ OKAY

The Mood Space

INDIA · SINGAPORE · MALAYSIA

ISBN 979-8-89186-965-3

Disclaimer

The information contained in this book is for general informational purposes only. While we strive to provide accurate and up-to-date information, the content may not always reflect the most current psychological standards or interpretations. This book is not intended to provide legal, financial, medical, or professional advice. Readers are advised to consult with professionals for specific advice tailored to their individual circumstances.

DEDICATED TO

you, dear reader:
thank you for holding
so many hearts in your hand

TABLE OF CONTENTS

CHAPTER 3 : POWER OF VULNERABILITY

LETTERS FROM A THERAPIST

CHAPTER 4: TRIUMPHING THROUGH TRIALS

LETTERS FROM A THERAPIST

CHAPTER 5: UNLEARNING AND RE-LEARNING NARRATIVES

LETTERS FROM A THERAPIST

CHAPTER 6: BRIDGING TO WHOLENESS

LETTERS FROM A THERAPIST

CHAPTER 7 : TALES OF SELF-DISCOVERY

LETTERS FROM A THERAPIST

ENDNOTES

THE FOUNDER'S NOTE

Dear Reader,

It is with great pleasure and deep gratitude that I introduce to you a compilation of powerful stories and personal journeys under the book title 'Shh we're ~~not~~ OKAY'. In reading these shared experiences of vulnerability, breakthroughs and transformations, I hope you find solace and inspiration as I have experienced.

When I embarked on the mission of starting an online mental health company, The Mood Space, I knew that I was stepping into uncharted territory, but I was driven by a shared vision—to create a safe space where people could find solace, support, and healing for their mental health struggles.

Today, as I reflect upon our journey, I am filled with immense pride and hope for what lies ahead. And while it's becoming more acceptable for us to talk about our emotions and seek help, there is still a significant stigma attached to mental health issues.

For far too long, societal norms and expectations have stifled conversations about mental health. The prevailing notion that we must be strong, stoic, and invulnerable has had a detrimental impact on countless lives. It has forced many to suffer in silence, battling their inner demons alone. But we refuse to let this continue.

This book was born out of a genuine concern for the well-being of people everywhere. We have challenged the stigma surrounding mental health and foster a community where people can openly share their experiences, fears, and vulnerabilities without fear of judgment or ridicule. We aim to empower people to embrace their emotions, seek help when needed, and take charge of their mental well-being.

I want to express my deep appreciation to the brave men and women who have shared their stories and trusted us with their vulnerabilities. Your courage is a beacon of light for others who are still searching for their path to healing. By opening up, you have shown that seeking help is not a sign of weakness but a testament to strength and self-awareness. I also want to convey my sincere gratitude to the entire team at The Mood Space. Your unwavering commitment and dedication has been instrumental in conveying the power of talk-therapy through the form of story-telling.

Together, we have created this book where people can find hope and healing. It is through such initiatives that we can continue to expand our reach and touch more lives.

Vidhi Merchant
Founder, The Mood Space

YES, YOUR NARRATIVE MATTERS

Within the story of your life,
You will find chapters of vulnerability and resilience,
paragraphs of pain and hope,
and sentences of transformation.

Your life story is a testament to your undying strength and belief in yourself,
sometimes wavering but always there.
YOU are the author of your story in this book called life,
YOU have the power to rewrite your narrative,
And, with each word,
YOU can redefine your mental health story.

Mahika Solanki

When was the last time you openly shared your story and felt heard?

For this World Mental Health Day, The Mood Space invited people to open up and share their Mental Health journey. Whether it's a story of a personal victory or a one of vulnerability, The Mood Space is here to hear them all, because every story matters.

Each story on these pages has the power to uplift others who may be going through similar experiences, reminding them that they are not alone. Publishing this book is our attempt to unite our community, supporting each other on our unique paths. As we read each other's stories, The Mood Space aims to build a generation that sees no stigma in seeking help for their mental health - a society, that wholeheartedly embraces mental well-being.

CHAPTER 1

CREATING SAFE SPACES

THERAPY GIVING YOU JITTERS? YOU'RE NOT ALONE!

My therapy journey has been truly enriching and supportive. My therapist has been very patient, and I have never felt any generation gap while communicating my worst fears and ugly thoughts. I still have a long way to go but I am already amazed by how this process has allowed me to see beyond my conditioning and take tiny steps towards a joyous life.

Thank you, dear therapist, for always listening, never judging, and, more than anything, for always telling me that it is perfectly fine to feel a certain way. Thank you, for helping me find the tools to navigate these feelings.

For anyone considering therapy or maybe contemplating it, if you're being held back by inhibition and fear, I would encourage you to take the step and start seeking professional help. Your future self will thank you for this brave step into building awareness and a deeper understanding of the why and how of your thoughts, emotions, and responses.

Selvarani Paulraj

MAN, I (HAVEN'T) GOT THIS!

I still remember the day I walked into my therapist's office as if it happened yesterday. My palms were clammy, my heart raced, and I had a lump in my throat as I contemplated sharing my deepest struggles with a complete stranger. Little did I know that taking that step would mark the beginning of a truly transformative journey.

I had been the 'man of the house,' and after months of fruitless job searching, I felt utterly worthless. Therapy turned out to be the lifeline I never knew I needed. It provided a sanctuary where I could slowly unravel the tangled mess of my thoughts and emotions. My therapist, with unwavering compassion, listened, validated my feelings, and gently guided me through it all.

Amidst tears, laughter, and countless "aha" moments, I began to understand myself in ways I'd never thought possible. With each session, I discovered my own voice, newfound strength, and a renewed sense of hope. Today, I am not the same person who nervously entered that therapist's office. Therapy has not only helped me heal but has also taught me the power of vulnerability and the incredible beauty of seeking help.

Anonymous

THE POWER OF CONNECTION

After several months of therapy, I came to a surprising and a somewhat confusing realisation – I had developed deep feelings for my therapist. However, this wasn't a typical romantic infatuation, but a complex, multifaceted one.

My therapist had become my safe haven, the person who listened to my innermost fears and dreams without an ounce of judgement. Their empathy and understanding allowed me to feel truly seen and heard in a way that no one else ever had. Yet, I was acutely aware that these emotions were intricate, and the boundaries of therapy were absolutely essential. So, my therapist and I worked together to use this experience as an opportunity for growth.

We engaged in open and honest conversations about these emotions, and my therapist provided guidance with grace and sensitivity. This unexpected experience became an integral part of my healing process, a way for me to understand the depth of my need for connection and validation.

Over time, my affection for my therapist transformed into a profound self-love and self-acceptance. I realised that my therapist had acted as a mirror, reflecting my own capacity for love and empathy. Under their guidance, I learned to redirect that love towards myself and others in a healthier and more balanced way.

Falling in love with my therapist may have been a complex chapter in my life, but it was a chapter filled with self-discovery and a profound recognition of the enduring power of human connection.

Anonymous

DECLUTTERING THE MIND

When I first began therapy, my life felt like an endless battle. I had been wrestling with the relentless pressure of deadlines, demanding bosses, and toxic coworkers for months. I felt utterly lost, with no one to turn to for help. I would sleep and wake up with work on my mind - My thoughts were as full as my Google Calendar. Then, one day, I reached a breaking point and realised I couldn't bear this burden alone any longer. That's when I made the life-changing decision to seek therapy.

I vividly recall stepping into my therapist's office, a mix of apprehension and hope swirling within me. I opened up about my struggles: the sleepless nights, the ceaseless anxiety, and the constant feeling of helplessness that had become my daily companion. To my surprise, this stranger, who is my therapist, welcomed me with a level of empathy and warmth I had never encountered before.

In the safe and nurturing space my therapist provided, I began to untangle the complex web of emotions that had been woven around my work-related stress. Together, we discussed coping strategies and techniques for establishing healthy boundaries in the workplace. Guided by my therapist's expertise, I made crucial decisions, including seeking a healthier work environment. With my therapist's unwavering support, I gradually but steadily discovered ways to manage my work stress and regain a sense of control over my life.

Anonymous

LETTER FROM A THERAPIST

Dear You,

I'd like to share a personal story that underscores the importance of counselling and therapy. Few year ago, I was contemplating seeking therapy, not solely because of personal concerns, but also out of curiosity to experience being a client.

"I'd like to reach out to Anupama and see what counselling is like. I've heard good things about her from our fellow classmates," I mentioned. Turning to my roommate, I asked, "What about you? Are you considering it too?" To my surprise, my roommate, whom I considered a close friend and a psychology student, responded, "Why should I go for counselling and therapy? I don't have any issues in life. You can go because you have family problems."

Her words caught me off guard. It was disheartening to hear such a response, especially from someone within the field of psychology. It felt like an emotional attack and a breach of the ethical principles within the mental health community.

However, after some time, we engaged in a conversation and reached a mutual understanding of her indifference and the source of her perspective. Life isn't always smooth sailing. It's filled with lessons and challenges, and we can't ignore the storms and thorns in both the present and the past. We acknowledged the ongoing effort required to maintain one's mental well-being, just as we care for our physical health. This experience taught us that counselling and therapy aren't limited to addressing specific problems. They also play a crucial role in personal growth and maintaining a healthy mind.

Sending support your way,
Maria Rose

LETTER FROM A THERAPIST

Dear You,

Taking the first steps on a journey towards healing and self-care can feel overwhelming. It's completely normal to have doubts and uncertainties, especially when it involves opening up to a therapist. However, it's essential to remember that therapists are compassionate professionals who are trained to create a safe and judgement-free space for you. Their primary role is to assist you in exploring your thoughts, feelings, and emotions as you navigate your inner world.

I can empathise with your initial hesitation to begin therapy. I too once wondered what I would discuss and believed I had my life under control. At the outset, therapy might seem like ordinary conversations, and you might even experience some emotional heaviness afterward. However, as the sessions progress, you may notice a growing sense of self-reflection. It's natural to occasionally feel overwhelmed during and after therapy sessions; this is part of the process.

Over time, therapy can empower you to find your voice and equip you with effective strategies to manage the challenges of daily life. The changes you'll observe may be gradual, but they are signs of your growth and transformation. Additionally, it's important to know that you have the autonomy to decide when to continue or discontinue therapy, ensuring that it aligns with your personal journey.

Think of your therapy journey as a car ride where you are the driver, and the therapist is there as your supportive navigator. Together, you can navigate any obstacles that may arise along the way. As you embark on this path of self-discovery and self-care, I want to wish you the very best of luck. Remember, you have within you the capacity to heal and grow, and therapy is a valuable tool to help you on your way.

Warmth & kindness,
Sanjoli Sakhuja

CHAPTER 2

FINDING HOPE

FROM DESPAIR TO DISCOVERY

In the depths of despair, therapy became a flicker of hope in my darkest hour. Lost in a sea of shame and self-doubt, I had convinced myself that I was unworthy of love and acceptance. My self-esteem had hit rock bottom, a stark contrast to my once-overachieving, hobby-filled life. But therapy proved to be a lifeline.

In each session, I delved into new facets of my identity, gradually reshaping my self-image. With every revelation, I regained a sense of control and self-worth. It was a journey defined by vulnerability and resilience.

To those who are considering therapy, I offer this advice: approach it with an open heart and an open mind. It just might be the key to unlocking your path to healing and self-discovery

Neha Linga

MY DIAGNOSIS DOESN'T DEFINE ME

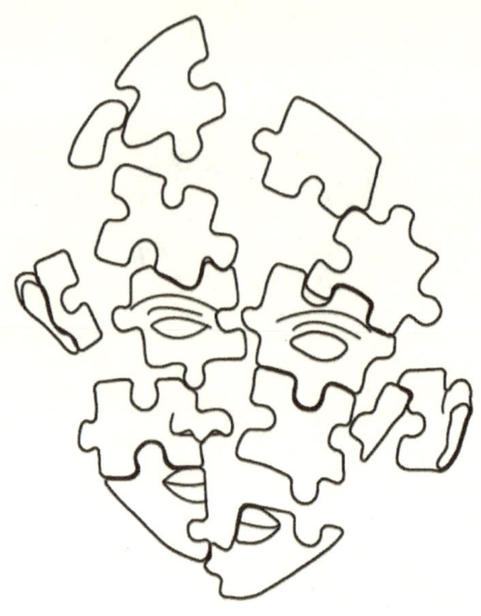

My journey in therapy began with a seemingly simple goal: to confront my OCD and address unresolved past issues. Yet, as I put these words together, I realise it's been an immensely profound adventure. It's been a journey of self-discovery, unlearning, relearning, and breaking free from patterns I unconsciously imposed on my relationships, work, and personal growth. In this quest, my therapist, Vishwa, has been a constant and reassuring guiding light.

Through this voyage, I've unravelled the intricate complexity of OCD, its profound links with anxiety, and its substantial impact on overall well-being. What strikes me most is how widely misunderstood and misused the term "OCD" is in popular discourse. But as I prioritise my mental well-being, I stand as a beacon of hope. I earnestly urge everyone to cast off the stifling shroud of stigma and approach mental health with the same compassion we offer to any other illness.

Vasantha Ganesh

I AM NOT WHAT HAPPENED TO ME

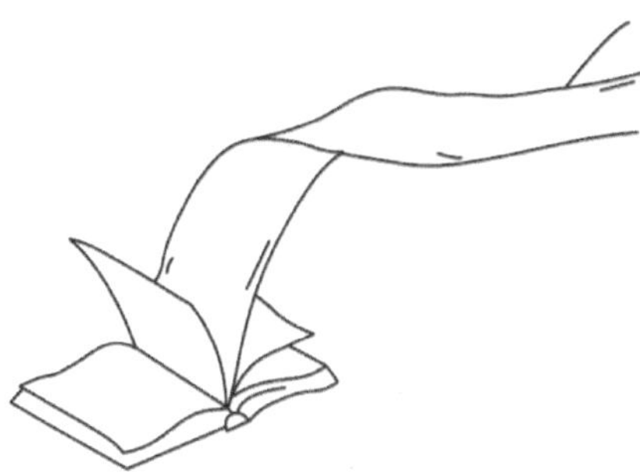

I come from a family with a controlling mother who was diagnosed with schizophrenia, and an emotionally violent father. My decision to seek therapy was driven by a desire to cultivate a healthy romantic relationship. Therapy, however, turned out to be much more than that – it helped me gain a deeper understanding of my mother's struggles. I came to realise that her insecurity about changes in her environment was a result of her condition, and this insight allowed me to approach her with compassion and not distance myself when feeling wronged by my father. I no longer harbour hatred for my mother, and I stand firmly by my decisions.

One of the most significant breakthroughs in therapy was my understanding of my "freeze response." I had endured sexual harassment from childhood into adulthood, never standing up for myself and shouldering guilt, believing I was somehow responsible for what happened to me.

I learned how the absence of protection from an adult during my early years left me feeling helpless, leading to a state of "freeze" as a response. Now, I've started to reconnect with my body and emotions. I can express my anger and disappointments in my close relationships, building healthy boundaries and nurturing loving connections.

My advice to others on a similar journey is this: Keep believing in your path to healing. Seek out a therapist who truly understands and supports you on your journey toward hope and recovery. Add more beautiful chapters to your story.

Nikita Gupta

DO YOUR BRAIN AND HEART QUARREL SOMETIMES?

Each day unfolds as a relentless struggle against the shadows of choices made long ago. A decade in the past, I walked away from a love that once embodied perfection, a love I believed to be my soul's true mate. My college boyfriend and I were like a match made in the heavens, a cosmic alignment too beautiful to last.

However, the harshness of reality intruded upon my dreams. A rigid caste divide drove a wedge between my boyfriend and me, shattering our lives. My parents, whom I deeply cherished, emotionally pressured me into marrying a man of their choosing. I yielded to their wishes, but in doing so, I crushed my boyfriend's heart.

My husband, a kind and caring man, endeavours to fill the void left by my lost love. He showers me with affection, respect, and everything I could desire. Still, I find myself drowning in a sea of remorse. Every touch from him makes me withdraw, for I recognize that he is not my soulmate.

I have become a fractured wife, unable to reciprocate his love, and a disheartening daughter, incapable of quelling my parents' disapproval. In my life, there are no villains; all, including myself, are victims of circumstance.

Yet, within my therapist's office, a glimmer of hope persists. She listens with unwavering support, guiding me through the tumult of my emotions, helping me navigate the guilt and yearning that clutch at my heart. I cannot say for certain if healing lies ahead for me, but I am committed to forging a future where my regrets do not define who I am..

Anonymous

LETTER FROM A THERAPIST

Dear You,

I understand and know that your path to well-being won't always be a straight road. It can often resemble a bouncy trampoline, with its own ups and downs. Throughout this journey, you'll encounter people, routines, and various elements that can lend you support. However, I understand that you may face moments when hope feels distant. And this is when having someone who can hold space for you can become invaluable. Initially, they might seem unfamiliar. But, they're trained, caring, and truly dedicated to creating a non-judgemental space for you that makes you feel safe.

In your sessions, they will extend empathy and care, and at times, they may gently challenge you when necessary. As you progress in life, you will face obstacles and moments of beauty along the way. However, with a trusted guide by your side, you can navigate through these challenges and learn to appreciate the good times. I genuinely understand that opening up can be daunting and sometimes, even a little frightening. However, I urge you to place your trust in the process – it's all about your well-being.

Remember, it's okay to be vulnerable, and seeking help is a sign of strength. Please don't hesitate to reach out and take that first step toward your well-being; after all, we all need support as we navigate this journey called life.

Always rooting for you,
Mehek Rohira

CHAPTER 3

POWER OF VULNERABILITY

EMBRACING YOU, UNAPOLOGETICALLY

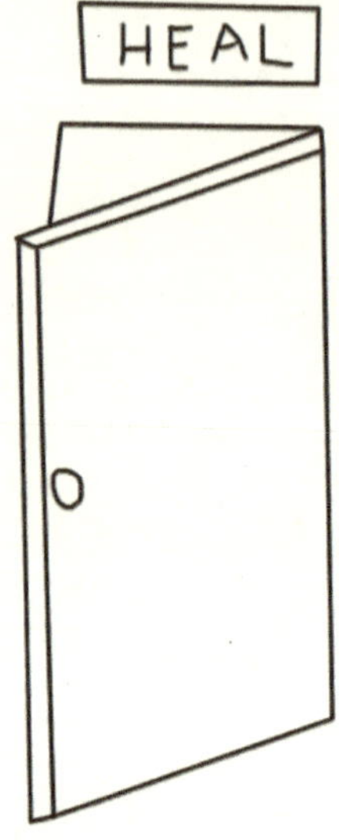

I can personally attest to how uncomfortable it feels at first when you start therapy. I too have been exposed to the false perception that seeking help represents weakness.

When I first started therapy, I was resistant and unsure about seeking support. I believed that not being able to manage my problems on my own, meant I was a dysfunctional adult. The beliefs made it hard to be vulnerable with someone about my difficulties. I discussed this with my therapist and she helped me realise why I felt this way. I learnt that I was available to take care of other people but found it hard to let other people take care of me.

I have had quite a few sessions now and am looking forward to growing and healing with the guidance and support of my therapist.

Anonymous

STRENGTH IN VULNERABILITY

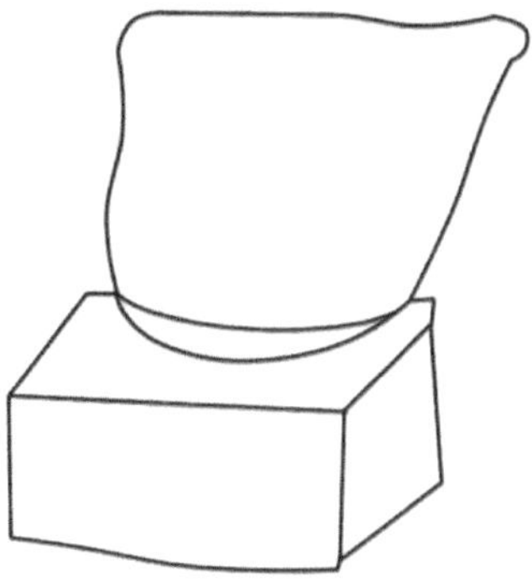

My therapy journey began when I found myself drowning in a sea of overwhelming emotions. My mother had passed away due to the pandemic. It was a sudden loss and my life had become a relentless rollercoaster, with tears and depression as my constant companions.

I took the courageous step to seek therapy, unsure of what to expect but desperately needing relief. As I walked into that therapist's office for the first time, I felt a mix of hesitation and hope. The therapist greeted me with a warm smile and provided me with a safe space where I could begin to make sense of what I was going through.

Through countless sessions, I learned to understand and embrace my emotions, no matter how difficult they seemed. My therapist patiently guided me through the labyrinth of my thoughts and so many tears, helping me develop coping strategies and a greater compassion for myself.

With time, I discovered the strength within me to face my demons head-on. I discovered the beauty of vulnerability. I realized that healing doesn't mean erasing scars but learning to wear them with pride.

My therapy journey has taught me that seeking help is a sign of strength, and sharing our stories can be a lifeline for others. I'm here to remind you that you're never alone on this path of healing.

Anonymous

UNEARTHING THE 'REAL YOU'

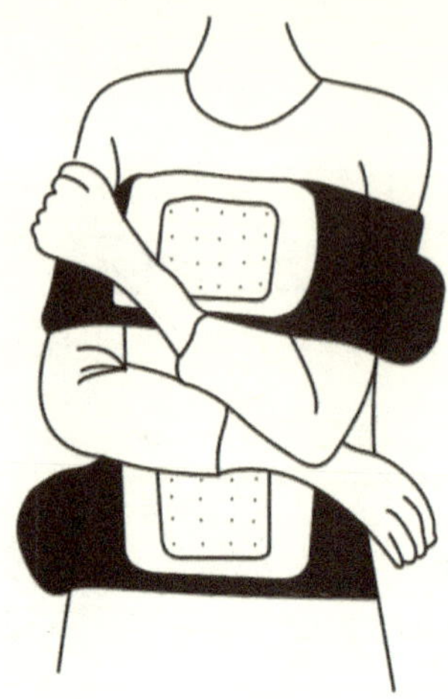

My first therapy session was shrouded in apprehension. I was there to confront my innermost fears and heal wounds that had been hidden for a long time. I cautiously allowed the therapist into the labyrinth of my thoughts. Weeks turned into months, and each session was a descent into the depths of my being, a journey through my past and a myriad of emotions that came with it.

Yet, within this vulnerability and fear, the beauty of therapy unfolded. It was a space where my pain met compassion, where my secrets found understanding, and where my silent battles were met with unwavering support.

I learned that therapy was not just about confronting the scary aspects of life; it was about embracing them and finding strength in vulnerability.

The beauty of therapy lay in the gradual emergence of my 'true self', in the realization that healing was possible and that I was not alone in my struggles. Even in the midst of fear of trusting someone I did not know, therapy, I realized could be the most powerful asset on the path to discovering the beauty within.

Anonymous

FROM HIDDEN FEARS TO HEALING

I've been carrying childhood anxiety without realising it. One fateful night, a minor disagreement with my best friend triggered a terrifying episode where my body and mind seemed to shut down, and my jaw locked. My hostel roommate rushed me to the doctor at 3 am, who diagnosed me with childhood anxiety and recommended therapy. That day, I experienced a debilitating panic attack, and my health deteriorated, leaving me in a constant state of fear.

During therapy, my therapist encouraged me to open up and express everything that was on my mind, urging me to confront my fears without inhibition. I also received advice to spend time with friends, which brought a sense of relaxation after the session. However, my closest friend of five years abandoned me due to pressure from his girlfriend, intensifying my fears and panic attacks. I became overwhelmed with a fear of everything around me – nature, people, places.

With time, I discovered the strength within me to face my demons head-on. I discovered the beauty of vulnerability. I realized that healing doesn't mean erasing scars Seeking help from a doctor again, they suggested a psychiatrist, but I hesitated out of fear. Eventually, I confided in another friend, who offered support and solutions. Sharing my problems with them provided some relief, and I'm now doing my best to cope.

This journey has taught me the power of sharing with both friends and therapists. Keeping mixed feelings bottled up can lead to overwhelming overthinking, making sharing an invaluable source of comfort and healing, but learning to wear them with pride.

My therapy journey has taught me that seeking help is a sign of strength, and sharing our stories can be a lifeline for others. I'm here to remind you that you're never alone on this path of healing.

Yashi

NAVIGATING LOSS WITH LOVE

The day my dog passed away, I didn't want to live anymore. His absence left a void in my heart. The house felt different, empty. Every corner held memories of his boundless energy and unwavering loyalty. I was drowning in grief.

My therapist's office became my sanctuary. I clung to his collar, a cherished relic, as I recounted tales of our adventures and whispered my deepest sorrows. Each tear that fell was a tribute to the love we shared. I longed for just one more tail wag, one more nuzzle, one more chance to tell him I loved him.

In therapy, I learned that grief was a journey, not a destination. It was a testament to the love we'd shared. Through the weeks and months of sessions, I began to heal. The pain didn't vanish, but it softened. I started to smile at the memories, to feel gratitude for the time we had together. My therapist taught me that healing didn't mean forgetting - it meant finding a way to carry the love forward. And so, I carry my dog's love with me, a warmth in my heart. In therapy, I found solace and strength, and in the midst of grief, I found a path toward healing.

Anonymous

LETTER FROM A THERAPIST

Dear You,

Brené Brown's insightful quote, "Vulnerability is not winning or losing - it's having the courage to show up and be seen when we have no control over the outcome," profoundly resonates with my journey as a therapist. My path has been marked by uncertainty and emotional openness as I've supported individuals carrying their stories filled with pain, doubt, and uncertainty. In these moments, I've shared their vulnerability, questioning whether my guidance alone could ease their suffering.

However, amid this shared vulnerability, I've come to understand that therapy is not a solo endeavour focused on "fixing" someone; it's a collaborative voyage where we walk hand in hand. It's about honouring your narrative and offering unwavering support as you navigate life's intricate twists and turns.

Therapy has gifted me the privilege of witnessing the authenticity and uniqueness of the human experience, coupled with our ability to feel, believe, and persevere in the face of overwhelming challenges, which continually astounds and fills me with wonder. As I walk alongside my clients, offering support in their quest to conquer these challenges, I hold deep admiration for their tenacity, which in turn inspires me to become a better version of myself on my own journey. The path to healing may be tumultuous, but it holds the promise of profound transformation and self-discovery. We are here to embark on this journey with you, to foster your personal growth, and to celebrate your achievements with you.

With the deepest compassion and unwavering support,
Ahana Ghosh

LETTER FROM A THERAPIST

Dear You,

Growing up no one ever spoke about mental health or the importance of taking care of ourselves aside from eating well and having some form of movement as a part of day-to-day life.

But when stressful situations occurred I could notice my heart begin to race, my palms becoming cold, and I feel breathless. And for the longest time, I thought I was alone in feeling this way. It was around this time that I stumbled upon Psychology as a subject and realised I was not alone in the way I was experiencing stress and that this did not make me weird or odd but it was just a part of being human, one that was not often spoken of.

Here began my journey of learning and understanding mental health and how it plays a role in everyday life, it was also on this path that I realised I wanted to make sure no one else felt the way I did, like an outsider, as no one would understand, and I began to take steps to become a therapist.

And while working with clients I can understand their apprehension to speak up, worried they might be judged, especially coming from a society like ours where speaking of matters of the mind involving feelings and emotions isn't always welcomed. But I have also had the opportunity to see my clients become more self-assured, more open to expressing themselves, and best of all; more content.

And this is when I knew that I had made the right decision all those years ago, in becoming a therapist. Nothing has been more fulfilling than providing a space where people feel comfortable enough to be completely themselves and express all that they have to hold back in front of the 'public eye'.

But I also understand that therapy is not always an easy process, to be vulnerable to a third person, even if they are a professional is difficult, and moreover being vulnerable with ourselves can be daunting. Therapy comes with its ups and downs, and sometimes it might be a trial and error process, but when you find your fit with your therapist and the space they offer, it can give back a lot more than we might have expected from it.

Sending you love & light
Priyanka TS

CHAPTER 4

TRIUMPHING THROUGH TRIALS

A JOURNEY OF TRANSFORMATION

In the midst of my battle with a brain tumour, therapy became a beacon of hope and healing. Sharing my concerns with a complete stranger wasn't easy at first, but it soon revealed itself as a transformative journey. Beyond assisting me in coping with my diagnosis, therapy equipped me with invaluable tools to navigate the daily rollercoaster of emotions and anxiety that accompanied it. Moreover, it provided a nurturing space for me to foster a deeper connection with my inner self, a connection that grew stronger with each session.

My story stands as a testament to the incredible resilience we carry within us, and it underscores the profound power of therapy in helping individuals conquer what may initially seem like insurmountable challenges. To anyone currently facing similar struggles, please know that reaching out for help can be the pathway to not only overcoming adversity but also to experiencing profound personal growth and enhanced well-being. Your journey may have obstacles, but with the support of therapy, you can navigate them towards brighter days ahead.

Anonymous

MY OCD DOESN'T DEFINE ME

Living with OCD was like having an uninvited guest in my mind. The constant need to double-check locks, wash my hands, or count things became overwhelming, and it felt like I was trapped in my own thoughts.

One day, after years of silently battling this internal torment, I decided to seek help. My therapist listened attentively and assured me that I was not alone in this journey. They explained the nature of OCD, helping me understand that it was not a flaw but a condition that could be managed. In therapy, I learned to confront my intrusive thoughts and resist the compulsions. It was challenging, but my therapist stood by me through it all.

With my therapist I went beyond the symptoms to understanding the root causes of the OCD, digging deep into my past experiences and traumas. I realised how interconnected my fears were with my emotional wounds.

My therapist provided a safe space where I could process these emotions and gradually untangle the web of anxiety that had ensnared me for so long. As the weeks turned into months, I noticed a transformation within myself. The intrusive thoughts still came, but they no longer controlled my actions. I could breathe a little easier, and life began to regain its colours.

Today, I am not entirely free from OCD, but I have learned to coexist with it. My therapist helped me understand that it was a part of me, but it didn't define me. The journey was arduous, filled with tears and triumphs, but it was a journey toward self-acceptance. I share my story with the hope that it inspires others to reach out and embark on their own healing journey, knowing that they too can find the strength to reclaim their lives.

Anonymous

FROM GUILT TO GRACE

Three years ago, I lost my closest friend to suicide. We'd been inseparable since our LKG days, and his absence left an unfillable void in my life. The pain was too much to bear, and I turned to alcohol to numb the relentless ache of his absence.

My therapist became my lifeline during those difficult times. I often found myself breaking down, tormented by questions like, "Why didn't I notice his depression? Why couldn't I save him?"

The weight of guilt was suffocating, but my therapist offered me a lifeline of understanding. Through therapy, I began to release the burden of guilt, session by session. My doctor encouraged me to honour my friend's memory by living a fulfilling life. We delved deep into my emotions, allowing me to confront the pain that had driven me to alcohol.

Gradually, I'm reclaiming control over my life. The haze of addiction is slowly dissipating, revealing the strength and resilience that have always resided within me. I'm learning to cherish the memories of my friend and value the precious gift of life.

While I may never fully understand the reasons behind his passing, I've found solace in my journey towards healing. The scars remain, serving as a reminder of the love we shared and the lessons I've embraced. I'm in the process of rebuilding my life, paying tribute to his memory by embracing each day, one step at a time, with the hope of reuniting in heaven someday.

Anonymous

UNBROKEN : MY CANCER JOURNEY

Cancer has cast a shadow of uncertainty and fear over my life. Facing the knowledge that I have less than five months left, has been an overwhelming experience, pushing me to the brink. Amidst the darkest moments of this journey, therapy has emerged as my lifeline. My therapist's unwavering support has been instrumental in helping me navigate the emotional turmoil that accompanies the relentless battle against this disease. In those moments of tears and occasional smiles, therapy provides a safe haven where I can process my fears and gather the strength to confront each new day. It serves as a poignant reminder that, even in the most daunting battles, we are not alone, and the human connection fostered through therapy can serve as a steadfast anchor for our souls.

I am 67 years old, and I am thankful that my granddaughter encouraged me to share my story here. To anyone who may be struggling, please don't hesitate to seek professional help. May God bless and guide each and every one of you on your journey.

Anonymous

LETTER FROM A THERAPIST

Dear You,

When life gets tough, and you're in the midst of a mental health crisis, it might feel like there's no way out. But here's an important thing to remember: Sometimes the only way out is - through. I know it's so much easier to distract ourselves and fall into our old, unhealthy patterns. But while you are doing that, you may be postponing the discomfort of facing & working through your issues and postponing your freedom from these struggles!

In the journey of life, challenges are the stepping stones towards wellness. They test our mettle, teaching us patience and perseverance.

Trusting the process is like tending a garden; we nurture the seeds of our well-being with care and patience. With each challenge we conquer, we grow stronger and more resilient, blossoming into the fullness of our potential. Through trust in the process, we find the path to lasting wellness.

As a therapist, I want you to know that we are here to help you through this journey. It's okay to feel sad, anxious, or overwhelmed. By going through them, you're making progress, even if it doesn't feel like it right now. Those tough emotions are like road signs guiding you towards healing. So, allow yourself to feel, to process, to grieve, for this is your sacred journey. And as a therapist, I walk beside you in spirit, whispering this gentle reminder:

Embrace the darkness, for it is in the depths that you discover your true light.

Sending support your way,
Ami Patel

CHAPTER 5

UNLEARNING AND RE-LEARNING NARRATIVES

TURNING A NEW LEAF

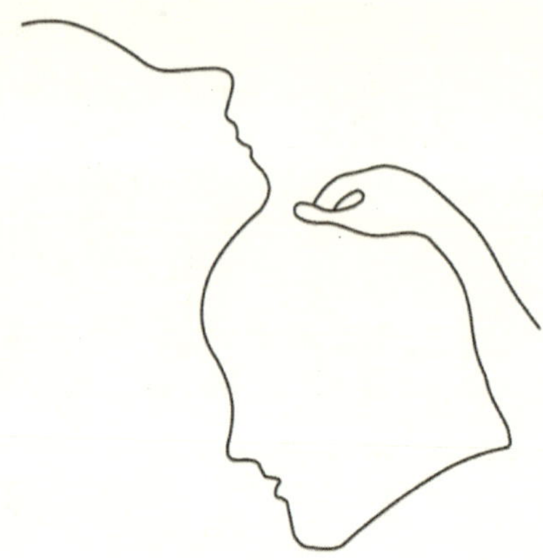

For years I have carried a painful secret with me. When I was thirteen, I experienced my first taste of love. We were mere teenagers, innocent and unworldly, and our "relationship" never went beyond stolen glances and secret smiles in the school hallway. When my father discovered the relationship he was consumed by anger and misguided beliefs and got my boyfriend killed.

Now, at age thirty, I find myself in therapy navigating the wreckage of my past. In our sessions, my therapist listens as I recount the haunting memories, helping me to release the pent-up emotions I've held inside for so long. She tells me, "Nikita, you were a child caught in a web of circumstances beyond your control. You mustn't carry the blame for your father's actions."

Through therapy, I'm slowly unravelling the knots of guilt and grief that have bound me. I've started to forgive myself, realising that I was powerless as a child. The stars that once symbolised my forbidden love are now guiding me toward healing and self-compassion. Though the scars remain, they no longer define me, and I'm learning to find peace within myself.

Anonymous

FINDING RESILIENCE WITHIN

For years, I was in a relationship that left me scarred in a terrible way. I was sexually assaulted by my partner at the time. The abuse had left my body feeling like a battleground. The mere touch of anyone, even my own mother, sent waves of panic through me.

This January, I embarked on a journey of self-discovery and healing. My therapist carried me when I felt like I had no ground to stand on. In our sessions, I recounted the painful memories, tears streaming down my face as I grappled with the confusion and guilt that had imprisoned me.

My therapist helped me connect the dots and understand that I had been a victim, not a willing participant in the abuse. She assured me that my body's responses were normal reactions to the trauma I had endured. Together, we worked on grounding techniques, mindfulness, and breathing exercises to help me regain a sense of safety in my own skin.

As weeks turned into months, the panic attacks reduced in intensity and frequency. I could finally embrace the idea of a body that was mine. While the pain will always remain, I'm learning to rewrite my narrative, reclaiming ownership of my body. Safety and healing are currently the new chapters of my life.

Anonymous

CHANGING MY HISTORY

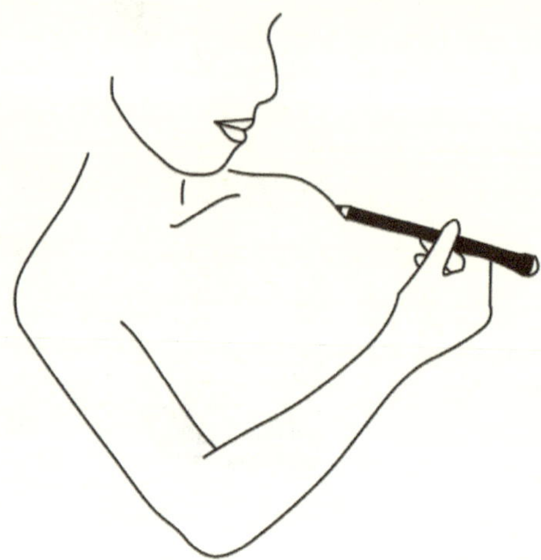

I am a housewife, and for years, my life has been an endless cycle of meeting the needs of my family. My days blur together, lost in the routines of cooking, cleaning, and caring for everyone else. My own desires and dreams have faded into the background like distant memories.

One day, I found myself sitting in my therapist's cosy office, my heart heavy with the weight of my self-neglect. Tears welled in my eyes as I finally confessed, "I don't even remember who I am anymore." But my therapist's warm and understanding presence put me at ease. "It's not uncommon for mothers and housewives to lose sight of themselves while taking care of others," she said gently. "Let's work together to rediscover the person you used to be."

My therapist helped me explore my interests and passions, urging me to set aside time for myself. "Self-carc isn't selfish," she reminded me. Slowly, I began to carve out moments for myself. I rediscovered my love for painting, something I hadn't done in years.

I learnt to communicate my needs to my family, helping them understand that my happiness mattered too. As I nurtured my own well-being, I noticed a change in my family dynamics. They became a little more supportive, realising that a happier me translated into a happier home. It was a transformation that I hadn't anticipated.

Through my therapist's guidance, I learned that taking care of myself was not a betrayal of my family but an essential part of being a better wife and mother. Through therapy, I gradually reclaimed my identity and started living a life that was balanced, fulfilling, and true to myself. I hope my story will be used to inspire other home-makers to make themselves a priority, as it is a common issue we face in India.

Anonymous

IT'S NEVER TOO LATE

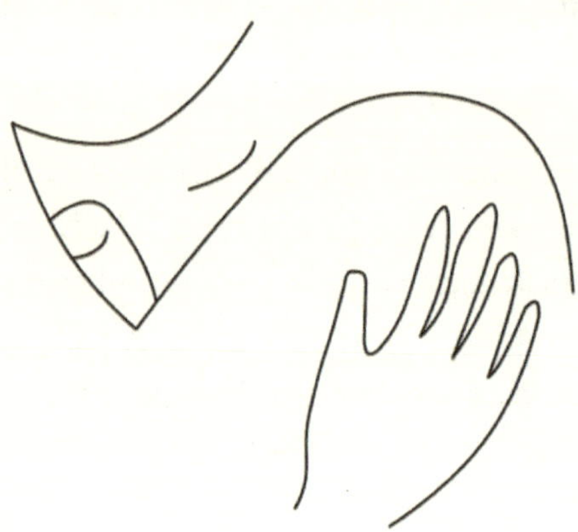

I always considered myself as someone who was quite emotionally intelligent and self-aware. I didn't think that therapy could offer anything new when it came to addressing the struggles I faced in my life. I figured I could manage on my own. But one day I finally decided to give therapy a try and I was stunned by the insights I gained in my sessions.

Through therapy, my restless, overthinking life has become a lot calmer. I have learnt a lot about myself and the patterns that have been part of my life for all these years. I genuinely wish I had taken therapy way back when a lot of the root causes of my current concerns had begun to emerge.

I am glad I finally did it, it's never too late.

Anonymous

AND STILL, I RISE

There was one defining moment that pushed me to book a therapy session. It was during a family gathering, a seemingly innocent conversation that spiralled into a heated debate about gender roles and expectations. As I passionately defended the importance of gender equality & women's rights, I was met with condescending remarks and outright dismissal from some family members. In that instant, the weight of years of frustration, alienation, and the constant battle to be heard crashed down on me. I felt isolated and overwhelmed, like I was speaking a different language.

It hit me then that my family's deeply ingrained beliefs were affecting not only my mental well-being but also my relationship with them. How can you love someone whose morality and opinion is so contrary to what you believe in? That's how they felt about me & I felt about them.

When I booked my first therapy session, it was my way of acknowledging the toll this had taken on me and recognizing that I deserved support in navigating these complex societal dynamics as they played out in my life. It marked the beginning of a healing journey, one where I learned to stand up for myself while also seeking understanding. Currently I live alone in my 2 BHK apartment with my dog and I've never been happier. My family has also come to terms with my life choices.

Anonymous

BREAKING THE CYCLE

Being the eldest daughter of a conservative Indian family, I truly believed that my family's honour rested on my shoulders. I was cautious of my words, my actions, my choices, even the way I dressed and presented myself in public. For a long time, I was content with being the 'golden child', until it started affecting my happiness. I booked my first therapy session on the day I experienced my first panic attack - I felt like my room was spinning and my heart was racing. I knew I needed professional help. Looking back, I wish I had begun therapy a lot sooner.

My life could have been completely different if I had learned how to say NO to certain things. I could have changed my degree from engineering to BBA, I could have ended that toxic relationship sooner. I could have avoided giving away pieces of my heart to many friends and family members who didn't know its value. My therapist made me understand that we humans deserve unconditional love. We deserve to get respect and care without working for it.

Through therapy, I have learned how to set boundaries, how to stand up for myself - even if it is scary, even if it means some people might dislike me. And for the first time in twenty-eight years of my life, I am feeling liberated and light. I am pouring my heart into self care and mindfulness. I am surrounded by new people who love me for who I am, with zero expectations. Can all this be a lucky coincidence, within a few months of therapy? I don't think so.

Anonymous

LETTER FROM A THERAPIST

Dear You,

If you find yourself struggling with a sense of stagnation, as though you're reliving the same story day in, day out, month after month, and year after year, you may have landed in the right place.

As a therapist, part of my role involves sharing the value of therapy and inner work. I do have concerns about coming across as overly preachy, as I sometimes advocate quite strongly for it. Some of this eagerness stems from my personal determination to persuade others to see things from my perspective. However, a significant portion arises from witnessing the benefits of self-improvement or, more accurately, working in harmony with oneself. In my own journey of self-discovery, therapy has often acted as a catalyst and a solid foundation.

Yes, even therapists seek therapy!

I was hesitant, much like anyone else. The prospect of opening up to a complete stranger was daunting. What if they judged me? What if they couldn't assist me? Most importantly, what if they thought I was too much to handle?

This hesitation was natural and didn't truly dissipate until well into my therapy experience. The desire to break free from repetitive, painful patterns consistently outweighed any reservations I had. As time passed, sharing my experiences and discussing my reality without judgement or dismissal clarified my story in my own mind and helped me move toward accepting it as my own.

Initially, I wanted to cherry-pick the aspects I embraced, keeping the attractive, shiny parts for myself while discarding the unpleasant ones.

However, with each therapy session and each moment of self-reflection that accompanied it, I grew closer to
embracing even the less appealing aspects. I made mistakes along the way, and I still wasn't the ideal self I aspired to be. But, before any transformation could occur, I needed to fully own my narrative and accept myself as I am. What we refer to as "unconditional acceptance" in therapy, became something I could experience first-hand. For the first time, it wasn't merely a theoretical concept; I was living it. To be clear, it's not always a smooth journey. There are days when it feels like I'm undoing my progress, taking two steps forward and four steps back. It can be challenging to remind myself that the work I've put in thus far still holds value. However, therapy and self-improvement are not so different from life in this regard.

Each day is unique, the circumstances change, and I may like some aspects while disliking others. The only way forward is through openness and acceptance—openness that isn't selective and acceptance that isn't conditional. Paradoxically, seeking therapy often begins with a desire for change, growth, and improvement, but the process begins with accepting and being at ease with who you are in the present moment.

This, in turn, becomes the foundation for self-improvement. The rewards on the other side of the hesitation to seek help are more profound than one can imagine!

With love,
Pratyakshaa Tewari

CHAPTER 6

BRIDGING TO WHOLENESS

WHEN PATIENCE PAYS OFF

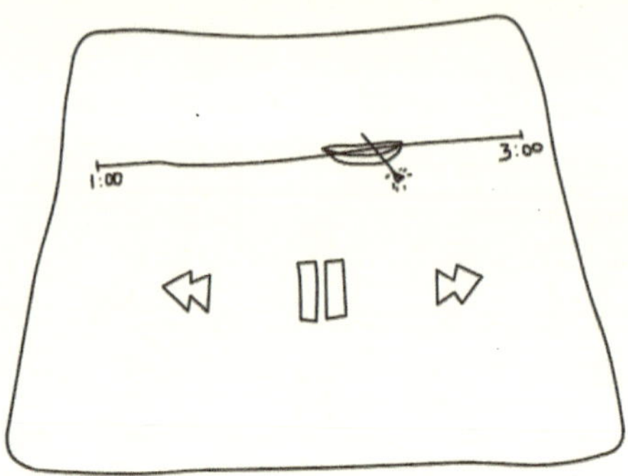

I came across my therapist through my workplace, and in the initial four sessions, I strongly contemplated parting ways because I didn't feel a strong connection. However, I couldn't muster the courage to end the therapeutic relationship, so I continued attending. Looking back, I'm genuinely grateful that I persevered through those uncertain early sessions. What I needed was a therapist, not a friend. It's often said that the right therapist is a matter of gut feeling, but for me personally, it takes time to build that connection, no matter who the therapist is.

I now realize that if I had given in to my initial impulse to leave, I might have fallen into a pattern of prematurely ending therapeutic relationships before truly giving them a chance to evolve. It was like skipping a song to go to the next and then the next one, without appreciating the beauty of the playlist.

Today, I'm working with a therapist who embodies empathy, non-judgment, and understanding. I'm genuinely relieved that I didn't abandon my healing journey prematurely. This experience has taught me the importance of patience and the value of allowing therapeutic relationships the time they need to unfold, ultimately leading me on a path towards greater wholeness and well-being.

Anonymous

REAWAKENING THE INNER YOU

Hello, I've been grappling with mental health challenges for the past four years, largely stemming from a series of failed relationships. About three years ago, I decided to seek therapy, and it did provide some relief. However, despite being diagnosed with clinical depression, I struggled with consistency in attending therapy sessions. It wasn't until last year, at my lowest point, that I discovered The Mood Space.

At that time, I felt utterly hopeless about life and wasn't taking my career seriously. With dedicated effort from both me and my therapist, I slowly began to see improvement. I vividly recall taking a selfie after nearly a year, a seemingly small act that still moves me when I look at that picture. Additionally, I found the courage to accept my circumstances and refocus on other aspects of life, including accepting a promotion that I had previously declined, believing I couldn't handle the new role.

There were several key insights my therapist helped me grasp:

- Setting small, achievable goals instead of fixating on the distant future
- Recognizing that we can only control our own thoughts and actions, not those of others
- Understanding that time is constantly evolving
- Embracing the idea that self-care is not selfish
- Acknowledging that I've been able to persevere and make progress despite numerous challenges

Some individuals may view therapy as a sign of weakness or a waste of time and money. However, I can attest to the profound benefits it can offer. Despite having an incredibly supportive network of family and friends, I felt the need for professional help. To truly benefit from therapy, one must maintain consistency, transparency, and trust in their therapist. Most importantly, it can only work if you genuinely desire it to.

To all those on their healing journey, I hope you find solace and recovery soon!

Anonymous

A LEAP OF FAITH

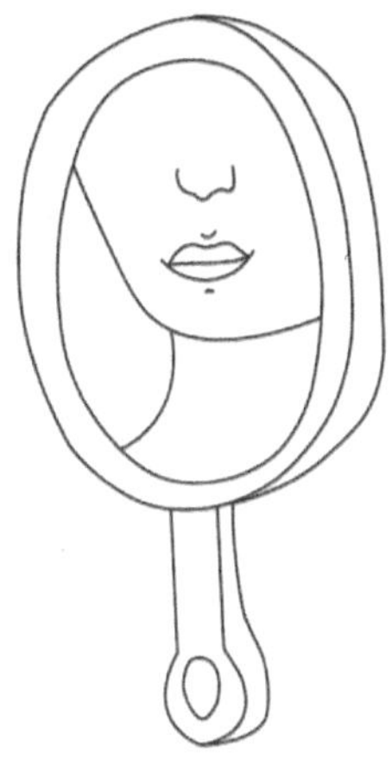

Entering therapy for the first time was a daunting journey into the unknown. It required me to delve deep within, where the answers to my questions lay dormant. At the outset, I was a shattered individual, emerging from a toxic relationship, with newfound revelations about the people I held dear.

Therapy became the mirror through which I could see my own narrative, recognizing how I had forsaken myself while striving to please others. ach session was marked by tears, but my therapist created a safe space where I could authentically be myself.

I am profoundly thankful to my therapist for guiding me out of one of the darkest phases of my life. It has now been more than two years of therapy, and in each session, I continue to discover a new facet of myself.

To anyone embarking on their own therapeutic journey, I want to convey this message:
I understand that it's a frightening step, but I encourage you to take it. Trust me, it will be a rollercoaster ride, filled with highs and lows. Yet, when you look back on this moment, you will be nothing but grateful to yourself for taking this courageous step toward self-discovery and healing.

Bhumika

LETTER FROM A THERAPIST

Dear You,

As a therapist I have the unique opportunity to witness courage and resilience on a daily basis. I have been on both sides of the therapy room. And both as a client and a therapist I have seen the powerful shifts that can happen in this space. But as wonderful as therapy is, I also know that some of us have had unpleasant experiences with it. We may have been in therapy sessions where we felt judged, had our concerns misunderstood or were suddenly left in the lurch halfway through the process.

A difficult therapy experience can leave a huge impact because it is one of the most vulnerable relationships we create with another human being. In therapy you share secrets and show parts of yourself that you have never revealed before. So, when it doesn't work out, you can feel hurt and betrayed. You may have even blamed yourself – telling yourself that you were responsible for things not panning out well.

For those of us who have had experiences like this, it is natural to feel a bit cautious about re-entering the therapy room. "What if it happens again?", you might tell yourself.

In many ways re-starting therapy can feel like going back to dating after a difficult breakup. Unfortunately, just like in relationships, there is no guarantee. To put it simply, you need to risk it to get the biscuit. But there are some things that can help you take this step. Spend some time figuring out what went wrong in the past therapy experience and what you want to change.

What are my goals and expectations from therapy? What were some gaps in the previous therapy sessions? What parts of the process made me feel uneasy or hesitant?
This allows you to get the most out of your next therapy experience.

And once you have this in place, share it with your new therapist! Your therapist will most likely want to hear about your previous experiences with therapy and how you felt about it. Us therapists believe that this conversation is necessary so we can ensure you feel safe and supported in therapy.

Even difficult therapy experiences can be opportunities for self-awareness and growth. So while I can't deny that taking therapy comes with certain risks, I can assure you that there is a lot that it can do for you if you'd like to try again.

Wishing you the best,
Riea Enok

CHAPTER 7

TALES OF SELF-DISCOVERY

UNVEILING THE REAL ME

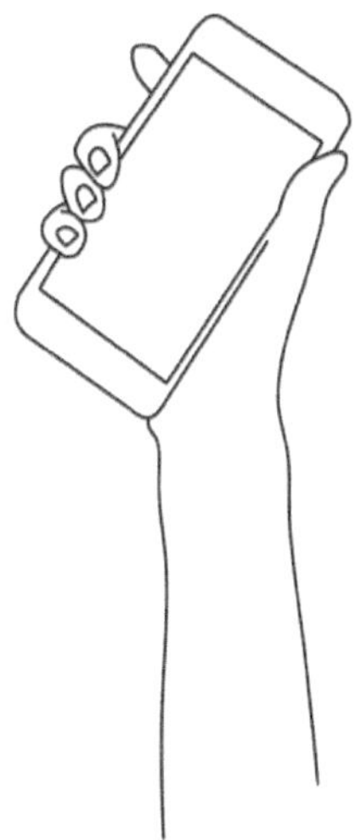

I discovered The Mood Space and began therapy during what was arguably the most challenging phase of my life. I had transitioned from the heights of happiness in the mountains to a state of profound sadness, bordering on thoughts of suicide. Strangely, there seemed to be no apparent trigger for this descent into despair.

After approximately six months of being immersed in this depressive fog, a dear friend gently nudged me towards therapy. Over the course of several sessions with my therapist, we delved into past childhood traumas, unravelled the complexities of family dynamics, and identified patterns of freezing during uncomfortable situations. I also learned about my "window of tolerance" and gained valuable insights into listening to my body and regulating my nervous system.

It's important to note that I considered myself reasonably self-aware, having engaged in significant introspection and soul-searching throughout my twenties. However, what therapy offered me was a fresh perspective through the lenses of psychology and trauma.

Once these areas were identified, my year of therapy unfolded as a journey of self-discovery in an entirely new light – a voyage that encompassed both my physical and mental being, as well as my conditioned thoughts and responses.

While it may sound cliché, therapy gave me back the most precious gift: my authentic self. For the first time in my life, I experienced the empowerment of adulthood. I was able to rebuild my relationships with my family on a foundation of mutual respect, without diminishing either them or myself. I gained the ability to recognize toxicity, gaslighting, and manipulation, and I found the strength to assert myself without surrendering my power. It was a revelation, and I have steadfastly held onto that sense of empowerment ever since. Once you uncover a truth within yourself, it becomes indelible.

To anyone contemplating the idea of seeking therapy, I urge you not to hesitate. The most difficult step is taking your phone out and reaching out for help. But - Take the leap, commit to a few sessions, approach it with an open mind, and be prepared to delve deep and do the necessary work. All you need to do is show up and trust the process, week after week, and I promise, you'll witness transformation.

I owe an immeasurable debt of gratitude to my therapist. That year of therapy was the most transformative period of my life, and its impact continues to show up through everyday of my life so far.

Pooja Ravi

REDISCOVERING STRENGTH

I'm a 19-year-old college student, and I received a diagnosis of chronic stress. The immense weight of assignments, exams, and the relentless pressure to excel had taken a significant toll on my well-being. Compounded by the responsibility of being the man of the house following my father's passing, I felt an added burden to achieve greatness in life. It was during this period that I decided to seek therapy as a means of coping.

My therapist and I embarked on a profound exploration of my anxieties, delving into their origins while equipping me with strategies to manage them. This journey was undoubtedly challenging, but with each session, I inched closer to healing.

My therapist's guidance emphasised the importance of prioritising my mental health and granting myself permission to step back when necessary. I began to grasp that life offers countless years ahead, providing ample opportunities for achievement. However, to realise those ambitions, I needed to be in optimal physical and mental condition.

Gradually, the suffocating grip of chronic stress began to loosen. I started to strike a balance in my life, making self-care an integral part of my routine alongside my academic pursuits. Additionally, my therapist encouraged me to contemplate the unfair societal expectations placed on men to be the sole breadwinners of their families, helping me recognize the social and economic roots of my stress.

The transformation I sought didn't occur overnight, but I'm steadily learning to navigate the challenges of college with newfound resilience. While my journey is ongoing, therapy has become my steadfast companion, guiding me as I regain control of my life, one step at a time.

Anonymous

NURTURING THE SELF

When I scheduled my first therapy appointment, I carried with me a lifetime's worth of burdens and a profound sense of loneliness. The weight of anxiety, the haunting spectres of past traumas, and the constant barrage of self-doubt had become nearly unbearable. But within the safe confines of those therapy sessions, I embarked on a journey of self-discovery that would change my life. My therapist, a beacon of empathy and gentleness, guided me through this transformation.

With each session, I began peeling back the layers of my emotional history, bravely confronting my inner demons. Tears flowed freely, but so did moments of laughter as I unearthed a wellspring of resilience that I had never before acknowledged. Therapy emerged as my sanctuary, a guiding compass through the tumultuous storms of life.

It's important to note that therapy didn't erase the scars I carried, but empowered me to heal and grow in their presence. Today, I openly share my story, not only as a testament to the transformative power of therapy but also in the hope that it may a door to someone overcoming their struggles.

Anonymous

SHAPING MY IDENTITY

As a young, dark-skinned girl in South India, I carried the weight of more than just my body. Years of childhood bullying had taken a toll on self-esteem, and I couldn't help but feel trapped within a body that seemed to betray me. My therapy journey began as a quiet, desperate plea for relief. My therapist welcomed me with kindness and understanding.

I began to lay bare the tangled thoughts and emotions I had kept hidden. I told my therapist about how I hated looking at the mirror and how I have never seen myself naked. I spoke of how I had never let anyone into my inner circle due to a fear of being judged and that no matter how many diets and workouts I tried, I continued to hate my body.

As I shared my pain, my therapist gently guided me to see the strength in my unique identity. She helped me understand that my skin tone held the richness of my heritage, and my body was the canvas of my life's experiences. Through our sessions, I started to mend the wounds inflicted by years of self-loathing. I realised my inner critic was actually the voice of my childhood bullies.

My therapy journey was raw and emotional. I had to confront the feeling of ugliness that had haunted me for so long. But with the support of my therapist, I began to see myself through a different lens. I was able to see the beauty and quiet strength that lay within me.

It was a transformation, not just of my self-esteem but of my soul, as I learned to embrace the colours of my own identity and love the body that had carried me through every moment of my life.

Nivetha Sekhar

LETTER FROM A THERAPIST

Dear You,

I hope this letter finds you in a moment of peace and reflection.

I want you to know that within you lies a beautiful story of transformation, waiting patiently to unfold. I wanted to take a moment to reach out and share some stories of hope, support, encouragement, and resilience with you. My aim is to demystify the therapy process and provide you with a sense of optimism and confidence as you embark on this journey.

Over the years, I have witnessed incredible transformations in individuals who decided to take the brave step toward seeking therapy. One such story that comes to mind is that of a client who initially felt overwhelmed by life's challenges but, through consistent therapy sessions, discovered their inner strength and resilience. As they navigated through their difficulties, they learned valuable coping strategies that empowered them to face adversities with newfound confidence.

In another inspiring instance, a client found solace in the safe and supportive environment of therapy. Through open conversations and guidance, they gradually embraced self-acceptance and gained a deeper understanding of their emotions. Witnessing their progress was a testament to the potential for positive change that resides within each of us.

It's important to remember that the journey towards healing is unique for everyone, and you are not alone in this. The therapeutic process is a partnership, and I am here to provide you with unwavering support, guidance, and a non-judgmental space to explore your thoughts and feelings.

As you continue your therapeutic journey, I encourage you to remain open to the possibilities that lie ahead. Every step you take, no matter how small it may seem, contributes to your growth and well-being. Your own story of transformation is waiting to unfold.

Life is a series of chapters, each filled with its own challenges and triumphs. Just as a caterpillar undergoes a metamorphosis to become a butterfly, you too have the potential for incredible change and growth. It's okay if you're feeling uncertain or even hesitant about the path ahead. Change can be both exciting and daunting, but it's a testament to your courage that you're open to the idea of transformation.

Think back to all the moments you've faced with determination and resilience. Those experiences, both big and small, have shaped you into the person you are today. Now, imagine what the future holds as you continue to learn, adapt, and embrace new opportunities for growth. It's important to remember that transformation is not about becoming someone else entirely, but rather a journey of self-discovery and self-acceptance.

As you move forward, know that you are supported and valued just as you are. Every step you take, every obstacle you overcome, brings you closer to the incredible story that is waiting to be told.

Embrace this chapter of your life with an open heart and an unwavering belief in your own potential. Trust that the challenges you encounter are stepping stones towards a brighter and more fulfilling future. Embrace the journey, for it is in the process of transformation that we often find our truest selves.

With kindness and encouragement,
Vishwa Modi

ENDNOTES

MENTAL HEALTH: A BRIEF HISTORY

In all of human history, there's a story as old as time itself—the tale of mental health, that has evolved over centuries. Long ago, people believed that mental health troubles came from evil spirits or the wrath of the Gods. Those who suffered were shunned, their voices silenced.

As time marched on, some societies realised that mental well-being meant finding mind-body harmony. They turned to meditation and a deeper connection with nature. But the shadow of stigma still hung heavy. People whispered about those who struggled, and the story of mental health remained tangled.

Then came the modern era, where science uncovered the mysteries of the mind. They revealed that mental health wasn't just about spirits—it was about how our brains worked, and it could be treated. Yet, sometimes, science made it sound too simple, reducing our rich human experiences to mere chemicals.

In the midst of change, a glimmer of hope emerged with psychotherapy. It put people's stories front and centre, a place where struggles and dreams could be shared. It was where people could rewrite their own mental health stories.

Across the centuries, mental health has transformed from a puzzling mystery into a story of resilience, recovery, and transformation. It stopped being a secret and became a shared narrative. People from all walks of life shared their stories, creating a vibrant world, and celebrating the human spirit.

And so, the story of mental health continues, shaped by voices and experiences through time. It's a story of learning and understanding, proving that human stories have the power to make sense of the once mysterious world of mental health.

CONCLUSION

Within each of us lies a multitude of stories, shaped by our unique life experiences and the world that surrounds us. These narratives play a profound role in shaping our interactions with the world and influence our emotional well-being.

When we open up and share these stories, especially in therapeutic settings, something remarkable happens. This act of sharing becomes a wellspring of hope, offering validation for our experiences and fostering a deep sense of belonging. Through this process, we embark on a transformative journey, one that encourages us to reconsider and rewrite the narratives we've held about ourselves and our mental health, while we rewrite the upcoming chapters of our life.

In this spirit, we entrust our personal stories of recovery to you, our readers. Our hope is that these stories serve as beacons of hope and sources of guidance along your own healing path. We aim to inspire you to reevaluate the stories you carry about yourself and your mental health, inviting you on a personal journey toward growth and fulfilment. Always remember, your stories hold the power to shape your healing journey and lead to profound transformations.

ACKNOWLEDGEMENTS

We would like to express our gratitude to those who have helped us bring this book to life.

First and foremost, we want to thank the awe-inspiring clients who have chosen to share their stories with the world. The power of this book is centred around your inspiring journeys. Your stories are a testament to the beauty of vulnerability, and the strength & courage that can be found in the darkest of times.

We would also like to thank our dedicated team at The Mood Space for pouring their heart and soul to bring this book to life.

'Shh, We're ~~not~~ Okay' was brought together by the efforts of the following:

Stories shared by **Clients in Therapy** across India

Editorial Team at The Mood Space

Content Editors: **Vrushti Oza & Mahika Solanki**

Expert Reviewers: Psychologist, **Riea Enok** & Chief Psychologist, **Vishwa Modi**

Creative Designers: **Rajalakshmi JP**, **Inseeya H Kaukawala**, **Aman Bheda**

Under the guidance of **Vidhi Merchant**, Founder

OUR SERVICES

The Mood Space is an online talk therapy platform meticulously crafted by experienced therapists. Our mission is to enhance access to therapy, destigmatize mental health, and provide carefully curated tools, thereby making high-quality mental healthcare accessible to Indians across the globe.

How we can help:

- Start Therapy
- Explore Corporate Wellbeing Services

Contact us:

SOCIAL MEDIA: @themoodspace

EMAIL: info@themoodspace.com

If you, or someone you know, is in need of support, please reach out to us.

Appendix:

At The Mood Space, we prioritise holistic wellness and believe that recovery goes beyond therapy. Introducing The Care Space, a carefully curated repository of wellness resources designed to support you on your healing journey.

Head over to our website now!

JOIN OUR CARE SPACE TODAY

www.ingramcontent.com/pod-product-compliance
Lightning Source LLC
LaVergne TN
LVHW041237150826
845673LV00008B/2414

* 9 7 9 8 8 9 1 8 6 9 6 5 3 *